A Crucified Christ in Holy Week

Raymond E. Brown, S.S.

A Crucified Christ in Holy Week

Essays on the
Four Gospel Passion Narratives

The Liturgical Press
Collegeville, Minnesota

The essays in this volume were originally published (under the usual
rules of ecclesiastical approbation) as follows:

"How to Read the Passion Narratives of Jesus," *Catholic Update* (April
  1984), which is the same as "Why the Accounts of Jesus' Death
  Differ," *St. Anthony's Messenger* 91 (#11; April 1984) 37–40.

"The Passion According to Mark," *Worship* 59 (March 1985) 116–126.

"The Passion According to Matthew," *Worship* 58 (March 1984) 98–107.

"The Passion According to Luke," *Worship* 60 (January 1986) 2–8.

"The Passion According to John," *Worship* 49 (March 1975) 126–134.

Cover design by Mary Jo Pauly

9

Library of Congress Cataloging in Publication Data

Brown, Raymond Edward.
    A crucified Christ in Holy Week.

    1. Bible. N.T. Gospels—Commentaries. 2. Passion
narratives (Gospels) I. Title.
BS2555.3.B763 1986   226'.06   85-24188
ISBN 0-8146-1444-2

Contents

Foreword

The passion narratives of the Gospels have been a research interest for many years, leading me to plan a full-scale commentary that would be a companion to my commentary on the infancy narratives, *The Birth of the Messiah* (Doubleday 1977; new enlarged edition 1993). In studying both these phases of Jesus' life my goal has been pastoral as well as scholarly: namely, to bring modern exegesis to the service of a Church that proclaims the infancy narratives in the Christmas liturgy and the passion narratives in the Holy Week liturgy. The Advent season that leads to Christmas and the Lenten season that leads to Holy Week are times of special emphasis on prayer and reflection and often include extra preaching services. My hope in writing on both infancy and passion narratives has been to supply ample material for reflection on both sides of the pulpit and to show that contemporary critical biblical research can be pastorally serviceable.

My commentary on the passion narratives covering the period from Gethsemane to Jesus' burial took over ten years of research. Entitled *The Death of the Messiah*, it appeared in 1994 (Doubleday) in two volumes and ran over 1,600 pages. I faced the same problem of length and time when I was working on the infancy narratives and *The Birth of the Messiah*; and I found an interim outlet by digesting some of my investigation in a series of popular articles appearing annually in the Advent/Christmas issues of *Worship*. These articles were collected in *An Adult Christ at Christmas* (Liturgical Press, 1978) which offered a simplified and digestible introduction to the comprehensive commentary. I have been following a similar procedure by publishing articles in the annual Lenten/Holy Week issues of *Worship* in which I treated the passion narratives of the Gospels. I am now making slightly edited versions of these four articles available under one cover, prefaced by an adapted general article on the passion narratives which I composed for *St. Anthony's Messenger*. Inevitably the format means that some major questions of historicity, sources, and non-canonical passion material must be left to the comprehensive commentary; but I hope that this brief work will enrich Holy Week for a wider number of preachers, hearers, and readers.

I dedicate this book to Monsignor Joseph Shenrock of the Diocese of Trenton, N.J., whose sixtieth birthday corresponds with the year of its publication. Classmate in the seminary and very close friend in the priesthood, to him I am indebted for many, many kindnesses over the years. Post-ordination theological education and active ecumenical involvement have enriched his parish ministry and created a pastoral context that should make this memento appropriate.

Union Theological Seminary (NYC 10027)

Foreword

General Observations on the Passion Narratives

Every year during Holy Week the liturgy of the Church exposes us to a bit of biblical criticism by appointing two different passion narratives to be read within a short period. On Palm or Passion Sunday we hear the Passion according to Matthew (Year A) or Mark (Year B) or Luke (Year C), while on Good Friday every year we hear the Passion according to John. "Those who have ears to hear" should notice that the two narratives which are read in a given year do not offer the same picture of the crucifixion of Jesus in either content or outlook. Let us consider the importance of that observation.

It has been argued that the gospel tradition was formed "backwards," starting from Jesus' resurrection and working toward his birth. Certainly early Christian preaching paid primary attention to the crucifixion and resurrection. For example, the Acts of the Apostles repeats: You killed Jesus by hanging or crucifying him, but God raised him up (2:32, 36; 5:30-31; 10:39-40). Then, as Christians reflected on the earlier career of the crucified one, accounts of Jesus' public ministry emerged, and eventually (in Matthew and Luke) accounts of his birth. Thus, a basic account of the crucifixion may have been shaped relatively soon in gospel formation.[1]

The shaping of such an account would have been facilitated by the necessary order of the events. Arrest had

---

[1] The majority of scholars hold this view, but a substantial minority thinks Mark put together the first consecutive passion account. This is often part of the thesis that exaggerates Mark's inventiveness in "creating" the Gospel format, a thesis that neglects the influence of OT prophetic "lives," such as the life of Jeremiah, which combines public actions, speeches, and a passion. Mark's passion account, however, need not depend directly on an earlier written passion narrative.

to precede trial, which, in turn, had to precede sentence and execution. The result in our canonical Gospels is a true narrative with a developing plot, tracing the actions and reactions not only of Jesus, but also of a cast of surrounding characters, such as Peter, Judas, and Pilate. The impact of Jesus' fate on various people is vividly illustrated, and the drama of the tragedy is heightened by contrasting figures. Alongside the innocent Jesus who is condemned is the revolutionary Barabbas who is freed, even though guilty of a political charge similar to that levied against Jesus. Alongside the scoffing Jewish authorities who make fun of Jesus as Messiah or Son of God is a Roman soldier who recognizes him as Son of God. No wonder that the liturgy encourages our acting out the passion narratives with assigned roles read aloud! Each passion narrative constitutes a simple dramatic play.

Indeed, John's account of the trial of Jesus before Pilate comes close to supplying stage-directions, with the chief priests and "the Jews" carefully localized outside the praetorium and Jesus alone within. The shuttling of Pilate back and forth between the two sides dramatizes a man who seeks to take a middle position, reconciling what he regards as extremes and not deciding for either. Yet the tables are turned; and Pilate, not Jesus, is the one who is really on trial, caught between light and darkness, truth and falsehood. Jesus challenges him to hear the truth (John 19:37); but his cynical response "What is truth?" is in reality a decision for falsehood. John is warning the reader that no one can avoid judgment when he or she stands before Jesus.

A. AUDIENCE PARTICIPATION INVITED

Personification of different character types in the passion drama serves a religious goal. We readers or hearers are meant to participate by asking ourselves how we would

General Observations

have stood in relation to the trial and crucifixion of Jesus. With which character in the narrative would I identify myself? The distribution of palm in church may too quickly assure me that I would have been among the crowd that hailed Jesus appreciatively. Is it not more likely that I might have been among the disciples who fled from danger, abandoning him? Or at moments in my life have I not played the role of Peter, denying Jesus, or even of Judas, betraying him? Have I not found myself like the Johannine Pilate, trying to avoid a decision between good and evil? Or like the Matthean Pilate, have I made a bad decision and then washed my hands so that the record could show that I was blameless?

Or, most likely of all, might I not have stood among the religious leaders who condemned Jesus? If this possibility seems remote, it is because many have understood too simply the motives of Jesus' opponents. True, Mark's account of the trial of Jesus conducted by the chief priests and the Jewish Sanhedrin portrays dishonest judges with minds already made up, even to the point of seeking *false* witness against Jesus. But we must recognize that apologetic motives colored the Gospels. Remember our official Catholic teaching (Pontifical Biblical Commission in 1964) that, in the course of apostolic preaching and of Gospel writing, the memory of what happened in Jesus' lifetime was affected by the life-situations of local Christian communities.

One coloring factor was the need to give a balanced portrayal of Jesus in a world governed by Roman law. Tacitus, the Roman historian, remembers Jesus with disdain as a criminal put to death by Pontius Pilate, the procurator of Judea. Christians could offset such a negative attitude by using Pilate as a spokesman for the innocence of Jesus. If one moves consecutively through the Gospel accounts of Mark, Matthew, Luke, and John, Pilate is portrayed ever more insistently as a fair judge who recognized the guiltlessness of Jesus in regard to political issues. Roman hearers of the Gospels had Pilate's assurance that Jesus was not a criminal.

Another coloring factor was the bitter relationship between early church and synagogue. The attitudes attributed to "all" the Jewish religious authorities (Matt 27:1) may have been those of only some. In the group of Jewish leaders who dealt with Jesus it would be astounding if there were not some venal "ecclesiastical" politicians who were getting rid of a possible danger to their own position. (The Annas highpriestly family of which Caiaphas was a member gets low marks in Jewish memory.) It would be equally amazing if the majority did not consist of sincerely religious men who thought they were serving God in ridding Israel of a troublemaker like Jesus (see John 16:2). In their view Jesus may have been a false prophet misleading people by his permissive attitudes toward the Sabbath and sinners. The Jewish mockery of Jesus after the Sanhedrin trial makes his status as a prophet the issue (Mark 14:65), and according to the law of Deuteronomy 13:1-5 the false prophet had to be put to death lest he seduce Israel from the true God.

I suggested above that in assigning ourselves a role in the passion story some of us might have been among the opponents of Jesus. That is because Gospel readers are often sincerely religious people who have a deep attachment to their tradition. Jesus was a challenge to religious traditionalists since he pointed to a human element in their holy traditions—an element too often identified with God's will (see Matt 15:6). If Jesus was treated harshly by the literal-minded religious people of his time who were Jews, it is quite likely that he would be treated harshly by similar religious people of our time, including Christians. Not Jewish background but religious mentality is the basic component in the reaction to Jesus.

General Observations

B. FACTORS IN THE DEATH OF JESUS

The exact public involvement of Jewish authorities in the death of Jesus is a complicated issue. Early Jewish tradition freely admits responsibility for "hanging" Jesus on the eve of Passover because "he seduced Israel, leading her astray" (Babylonian Talmud, *Sanhedrin* 43a). Yet modern Jewish writers have rejected in whole or in part Jewish involvement in the crucifixion. A frequent argument is that the Sanhedrin legal procedures described in the Gospels do not agree with Jewish Law expounded in the Mishnah and so cannot be factual. The Mishnah, completed about A.D. 200, is the written codification of the *Pharisee* oral law; but in Jesus' time Sadducee priests, not Pharisees, dominated the Sanhedrin, and they rejected oral law, claiming to rely only on the written law of the OT. The trial of Jesus as narrated in the Gospels does not violate the letter of the written law; therefore, the accounts of Jewish involvement cannot be so easily dismissed on technical grounds.[2] We are reminded by this point, however, that, although during his ministry Jesus may have argued with the Pharisees, those Jews who had the most direct involvement in his death were the priests, perhaps angered by his prophetic castigation of Temple practice.

Let us probe further, asking in what way and to what extent the priests and the Sanhedrin were involved. A

[2] Other explanations exonerating Jewish religious leadership posit two Sanhedrins, e.g., one political which worked with the Romans (and which found Jesus guilty at their bidding) and the other religious (which did not deal with Jesus or was not opposed to him). The evidence for the existence of such diverse bodies is slim; and those who shaped early Christian tradition (among whom some were certainly familiar with the Palestinian scene) make no such distinction. The oldest preserved Christian writing (*ca.* A.D. 50), I Thessalonians, speaks baldly about "the Jews who killed the Lord Jesus" (2:14-15—a text that is probably authentically Pauline despite attempts to classify it as a later scribal edition). Such a sentiment may be overgeneralized, but it is scarcely without some foundation in fact.

General Observations

13

distinguished Jewish commentator on the trial of Jesus, Paul Winter, would give priority to Luke's account of the procedure against Jesus, for, unlike Mark and Matthew, Luke reports no calling of witnesses and no Jewish death sentence on Jesus. Yet the failure to mention a death sentence probably does not mean that in Luke's mind the Jewish leaders were free from responsibility for the death of Jesus, since elsewhere he stresses an active Jewish role (Acts 2:36; 4:10; 5:30; 7:52; 10:39; 13:27-29). Nevertheless, unlike the formal Sanhedrin trial at night recounted in Mark and Matthew (with the latter specifying the high priest to have been Caiaphas), in Luke there is a less formal Sanhedrin questioning of Jesus in the morning. John recounts no Sanhedrin session after the arrest of Jesus but only a police interrogation conducted by the high priest Annas (18:19-24). Further confusion: John 18:3, 12 indicates that the party which arrested Jesus involved not only Jewish police supplied by the high priest but also Roman soldiers with their tribune. Roman soldiers would not have taken part without the prefect's permission or orders; and so, if the Johannine information is historical, Pilate had to have known beforehand about the arrest of Jesus and perhaps had even commanded it.

It is not impossible that, having heard rumors of Jesus as the Messiah (the anointed king of the house of David whom many Jews were awaiting), Pilate wanted the Jewish authorities of the Sanhedrin to investigate him and so assisted in his arrest. Some of those authorities would have had their own religious worries about Jesus and antipathies toward him (for example, as a false prophet). Yet they could have told themselves that they were only carrying out orders in handing Jesus over to the Romans for further action, on the grounds that under interrogation he had not denied that he was the Messiah. (Notice, I say "not denied," for the response of Jesus to the question of

General Observations

being the Messiah differs in the various Gospel accounts of the trial: "I am" in Mark; "That is what you say, but . . . ." in Matthew; "If I tell you, you will not believe" in Luke; see John 10:24-25.) Religious people of all times have accomplished what they wanted through the secular authority acting for its own purposes.

Attention must be paid to such complications lest the liturgical reading of the passion narratives lead to simplistic accusations about guilt for the death of Jesus. As I shall point out when I discuss the individual passion accounts, both Matthew ("all the people" in 27:25) and John ("the Jews" throughout) generalize hostilely, so that participation in the execution of Jesus is extended beyond even the Jewish leadership. Reflective of this, some famous Christian theologians (Augustine, John Chrysostom, Thomas Aquinas, Martin Luther) have made statements about the Christian duty to hate or punish the Jews because they killed the Lord. Thus, modern apprehensions about the anti-Jewish impact of the passion narratives are not groundless. One solution that has been proposed is to remove the "anti-Semitic" passages from the liturgical readings of the passion during Holy Week, a type of "Speak no evil; see no evil; hear no evil" response. But removing offensive passages is a dangerous procedure which enables hearers of bowdlerized versions to accept unthinkingly everything in the Bible. Accounts "improved" by excision perpetuate the fallacy that what one hears in the Bible is always to be imitated because it is "revealed" by God, and the fallacy that every position taken by an author of Scripture is inerrant.[3] In my opinion, a truer response is to continue to read unabridged passion ac-

---

[3] How much more cautious is Vatican II (Dogmatic Constitution *Dei verbum* on Divine Revelation, #11) in confining inerrancy: "The books of Scripture must be acknowledged as teaching firmly, faithfully, and without error that truth which God wanted put into the sacred writings for the sake of our salvation."

General Observations

counts in Holy Week, not subjecting them to excisions that seem wise to us—but once having read them, to preach forcefully that such hostility between Christian and Jew cannot be continued today and is against our fundamental understanding of Christianity. Sooner or later Christian believers must wrestle with the limitations imposed on the Scriptures by the circumstances in which they were written. They must be brought to see that some attitudes found in the Scriptures, however explicable in the times in which they originated, may be wrong attitudes if repeated today. They must reckon with the implications inherent in the fact that God has revealed *in words of men.* Congregations who listen to the passion proclamations in Holy Week will not recognize this, however, unless it is clearly pointed out. To include the passages that have an anti-Jewish import and not to comment on them is irresponsible proclamation that will detract from a mature understanding of our Lord's death.

C. HOW DID JESUS HIMSELF VIEW HIS DEATH?

Besides reflecting on what the passion of Jesus should mean for us, we may ask what did it mean for Jesus? We are told in Romans 4:25 that Jesus died for our sins, but would Jesus himself have used such language? Did he foresee the exact manner of his death and victory? In Mark (8:31; 9:31; 10:33-34, with parallels in Matt and Luke) there are three predictions of the fate of the Son of Man, one more detailed than the other. Yet, once we recall the Catholic Church's official teaching that sayings uttered by Jesus have been expanded and interpreted by the apostolic preachers and the evangelists before they were put in the Gospels, we have the right and duty to ask whether these predictions have not become more exact by hindsight. Have they not been filled out with details by those who knew what happened to Jesus? John has

General Observations

16

three statements (3:14; 8:28; 12:32, 34) about the "lifting up" of the Son of Man—a much less precise reference to crucifixion and ascension! Jesus may have originally expressed general premonitions about his suffering and death (a hostile fate discoverable from the example of the prophets), plus a firm trust that God would make him victorious (without knowing exactly how).

Hebrews 5:7-8 reports, "In the days when he was in the flesh, he offered prayers and supplications with cries and tears to God who was able to save him from death, and he was heard because of his reverence. Son though he was, he learned obedience from what he suffered." Jesus had preached that God's Kingdom would be realized most readily when human beings acknowledged their dependence on God. The model for this Kingdom was not power over others but the helplessness of the little child. We humans come most clearly to terms with our helplessness when we face death. Did Jesus, the proclaimer of the Kingdom, himself have to experience the vulnerability of dying before the Kingdom could be achieved in and through him? Jesus' reference at the Last Supper (Luke 21:16, 18) to the imminence of the Kingdom confirms the possibility that he used "Kingdom" language to phrase his own understanding of his death. The coming of the Kingdom would involve the ultimate destruction of the power of evil, and Jesus' confrontation with Satan in the great period of trial is echoed in various passion narrative passages (Mark 14:38; Luke 22:53; John 14:30). The thought of such a confrontation may explain Jesus' anguish before his fate; and his trust in God's power to defeat Satan may have been his way of expressing the truth caught by NT writers when they said that he died to remove sin.

General Observations

D. EARLY CHRISTIAN VIEWS OF JESUS' DEATH

Finally, we should reflect on what Jesus' passion meant to Christians of the NT period, using the Gospels as a guide. It is noteworthy that many features depicted by later artists and writers have no place in the Gospel accounts, for instance, elements of pathos and emotion, and a concentration on pain and suffering. On Calvary, the evangelists report laconically, "They crucified him," without reference to the manner. Strikingly, however, they pay attention to the division of his garments and to the exact placement of the criminals crucified with him. Such details were important to the early Christians because they found them anticipated in OT psalms and prophets. Not biography but theology dominated the choice of events to be narrated, and the OT was the theological source-book of the time. (This approach is far more likely than the skeptical contention that Christians created the details of the passion in order to fulfill the OT.) The evangelists were emphasizing that through the Scriptures of Israel God had taught about His Son. Their emphasis also had an apologetic touch against Jews who rejected the crucified Jesus precisely because they did not think he fulfilled Scriptural expectations.

Moving beyond the shared Christian theology of the passion, we come now to the distinctive insight in the passion account of each canonical Gospel. The subsequent chapters of this small book will be devoted consecutively to each of the four accounts, and in a conclusion I shall make a brief overall comparison. As I stated in the Foreword, my goal is to enrich Holy Week preaching and reflection on the passion accounts; but let me note two ways in which scholarly practicality forces me to deviate slightly from the lectionary passion narratives read on Palm/Passion Sundays and on Good Friday. (1) The liturgical readings extend from the Last Supper to the

General Observations

burial.[4] In point of fact scholars debate about where the passion narrative begins and ends (either as a separate entity originating before the written Gospels or as intended by the individual evangelists). Does it begin with the Last Supper and does it include the women's visit to the empty tomb? In I Corinthians Paul speaks of a tradition of eucharistic words and actions "on the night when Jesus was handed over" (11:23) and of a tradition that Christ died and was buried, was raised and appeared (15:3). Perhaps, then, there was already a pre-Pauline sequence from the eucharist to the tomb. Certainly Luke thought of the Last Supper, the arrest, the passion and death, the burial, and the visit to the tomb as a unit. (He situates the prediction of Peter's denials at the supper, tying the supper into what follows; similarly, after the burial he has the women prepare the spices that they bring to the tomb on Sunday morning.) Mark, however, may have joined separate traditions of the supper, the passion (beginning with the scene in Gethsemane), and the empty tomb. A scholar might wish to subdivide a commentary on Matthew so that the passion section begins with 26:1, or with 26:30, or with 26:36! Be that as it may, in reflecting on the passion in Holy Week we must be practical. Sections of the Gospels dealing with the Last Supper (containing the eucharistic institution) and with the resurrection are extremely complicated from a scholarly viewpoint. Even the long, comprehensive commentary that I hope to produce could not treat those sections within the confines of one volume. Moreover, in our ordinary understanding of liturgical topics, the Last Supper belongs to Holy Thursday preaching, and the resurrection belongs to Easter Sun-

---

[4] This is the range of the "long form." There are short forms (which throughout the Missal are an abomination to be avoided at all costs), but these eliminate parts of the story that must be considered essential in any comprehensible understanding of the passion.

General Observations

day and afterwards. One would not normally make those the subject of passion preaching and reflection associated with Palm/Passion Sunday and Good Friday. Thus, a manageable and intelligible definition of the passion narrative as extending *from Gethsemane to the grave* will be operative in this book (and in my future *The Death of the Messiah*). In each case, however, I shall try to situate the passion so-defined into the larger context of the individual Gospel so that the evangelist's intent and flow of thought are not neglected.

(2) Within the pattern of A, B, and C years, the liturgy of Palm/Passion Sunday presents the Synoptic passion narratives in the order Matthew, Mark, and Luke, so that the Matthean narrative is read first, a year before the Marcan narrative. Although a few scholars (who are persistent and vocal) would have Mark dependent upon Matthew and Luke, the majority opinion by far is that both Matthew and Luke drew on Mark. In the passion narrative in particular, Matthew is so close to Mark that there is no need to posit another additional source. Apparently the author of Matthew edited and adapted what he drew from Mark, adding a few items from popular tradition and early Christian apologetics, for example, about the death of Judas, about Pilate (washing his hands) and Mrs. Pilate (dreaming about Jesus' innocence), and about guards placed at the tomb. The interdependence of the canonical passion accounts is not a matter of great importance for the essays in this volume, for I am deliberately concentrating on the distinctive outlook offered by each evangelist and not on where the evangelist got his ideas. Nevertheless, a sequence in which Mark is placed first will give a clearer understanding of the passion to someone who reads the four Gospel essays consecutively. It seems then that nothing will be lost and something may be gained if I use the order Mark, Matthew, Luke, and John.

General Observations

The Passion According to Mark

The Marcan passion narrative is read on Palm/Passion
Sunday in the same liturgical year (B) in which the Gospel
of Mark has supplied the readings on the Sundays of the
Ordinary Time. In connecting these two Marcan contribu-
tions, the Church is recognizing that the evangelist does
not present his story of Jesus' death without having
prepared for it in the narrative of the public ministry. At
the very beginning of Mark (1:14) John the Baptist was
"handed over" to Herod, who eventually yielded to
pressure by others and killed this prophet (6:26). Facing
the question of who Jesus might be, Herod evoked the
violent death of John: "John whom I beheaded has been
raised" (6:16). When Jesus' ministry in Galilee had just
begun, Mark (3:6) tells us that Pharisees and Herodians
plotted to destroy him. Three times Jesus had predicted
his own violent death (8:31; 9:31; 10:33-34); yet his
disciples never understood. All of this came to a head
when Jesus arrived at Jerusalem and purified the Temple,
declaring that it must be a house of prayer for all the
nations—that led the priests and the scribes in Jerusalem
to plot to destroy him (11:17-18). In this threatening situation, a woman who admired Jesus prepared him for death
by anointing his body for burial (14:3-9), but one of his
intimates among the Twelve conspired to hand him over
to the priests who were his enemies (14:1-2, 10-11). Knowing of this treason (14:21), Jesus at the Last Supper was
willing to pour out his blood for all as a sign of the cove-
nant that God was making anew with His people (14:24).

A. GETHSEMANE: PRAYER AND ARREST (14:26-52)
Thus, the Jesus who left the supper room to go with his

disciples to the Mount of Olives[5] was one who had come
to terms with the necessity that he must suffer and die
before the Kingdom of God could come. In the Marcan
view, however, the disciples had not accepted that reality.
Accordingly, Jesus' words to them institute a tragic
message: all will be scattered (14:27). Peter denies this,
only to be told that he will be particularly unfaithful, denying Jesus three times. The Marcan passion begins on
this gloomy note, and the darkness will intensify until
Jesus breathes his last the next day. In all that time no
support will come from those who have been his
followers, and he will die alone. The tragedy seems almost
too much for Jesus himself. Having separated from the
larger body of the disciples and then further separated
from Peter, James, and John, Jesus confesses plaintively,
"My soul is very sorrowful, even to death" (14:34).
Previously Jesus had affirmed, "Whoever would save his
life will lose it"; but now, more insistently than in the
other Gospels, he prays that this hour or this cup might
pass from him. Even though he has predicted Peter's
denials, he is upset that Peter could not watch one hour
with him. Although there is no direct response from God
to Jesus' prayer for deliverance, ultimately Jesus rises
resolved to encounter the betrayer, leaving us to assume
that he has understood God's answer to be that he must
drink the cup and face the hour that is at hand.

For Mark (and here he differs from the other three
evangelists) Jesus' resignation to his fate may be seen in
his failure to respond to the Judas who kisses him or to
the bystander who draws the sword and strikes the slave
of the high priest on the ear. If the hour and cup could
not pass, as Jesus had prayed earlier, let be what God
wills. And so when Jesus is arrested, his last words are,

---

[5] The symbolism of this place will be treated in relation to Matthew's account
which develops the Davidic connections of the site.

Marcan Passion Narrative

"Let the Scriptures be fulfilled." Seeing such resignation, the disciples all forsake him and flee.

Once again differing from the other evangelists, Mark underlines almost brutally the totality of the abandonment. He tells the story of a young man who does seek to follow; but, when seized as Jesus had been, this would-be disciple leaves in the hands of his captors the linen garment that had clothed him, and runs away naked. Some scholars have sought to relate this figure to the young man who after the resurrection will sit at the empty tomb clothed in a white robe. Among the symbolisms suggested is that of the Christian who descends naked into the baptismal water to die with Jesus and then comes forth to be clothed in a white robe. Probably such symbolism lies beyond Mark's intention. Rather, the disciple fleeing naked is symbolic simply of the total abandonment of Jesus by his disciples. The first disciples to be called left nets and family (1:18, 20), indeed everything (10:28), to follow him; but this last disciple, who at first sought to follow Jesus, ultimately leaves everything to get away from him.

The stark Marcan portrayal of Jesus at Gethsemane has been recognized as difficult both by believers and nonbelievers. Well-meaning preachers and writers have argued that Jesus' sorrow was not in the face of death and that he did not ask to be delivered from suffering; rather, foreseeing all the sin in the world, he shrank at the thought of so much evil. More perceptively, anti-Christian critics have recognized that Mark was indeed describing a reaction to death; but they queried how a Jesus who so feared to die could be divine, or how one so devoted to God could ask to avoid the cross that he proclaimed as necessary for others. Even in recent times the picture of a Jesus distressed and greatly troubled, asking to be delivered, has been contrasted with a Socrates calmly accepting death as a deliverance from this world of shadowy realities and as an entrée to a better world. All of this fails to consider the basic outlook on death inherited from the OT. In the theology of Genesis, human beings were created to enjoy God's presence in this life and not to die. Death was an evil imposed on Adam and Eve, and ultimately in Israelite thought it came to be seen as a realm of alienation from God. The NT, even after Christ's victory, speaks of death as the last enemy to be overcome (1 Cor 15:26). For Jesus, the struggle with death is part of the great trial or temptation of the last times; and he is faithful to Judaism when he tells his disciples to pray not to enter into this temptation (Mark 14:38). Their great danger is that the trial comes at a moment when they do not expect and are not watching (13:34-37), and so Jesus warns them to watch. It is not surprising that either ancients or moderns imbued with platonic ideals would find Jesus' attitude toward death disgraceful. The Christian answer lies not in underplaying the apprehension of Jesus, but in stressing the importance of life in this world so that death is seen as a distortion and not as a welcome deliverance—an enemy that, because of Jesus' victory, cannot conquer but an enemy nonetheless. The obedience that Jesus showed to God's will and the trust that this demanded of him are all the more impressive when it is realized how satanic an enemy he was encountering.

B. SANHEDRIN TRIAL; PETER'S DENIAL (14:53-72)

Mark establishes a transition from Gethsemane by two sentences, each giving the scenario for an episode to take place this night. The first sentence (14:53) has Jesus led before the assembly of chief priests, elders, and scribes— the Jewish Sanhedrin, which even under Roman occupation, had certain governmental and judicial functions. The second sentence (14:54) has Peter follow Jesus into the

Marcan Passion Narrative

courtyard of the high priest, where he sits with guards, warming himself at the fire. Jesus will be questioned before the Sanhedrin and Peter will be questioned in the courtyard; the behavior of the two men will form a sharp contrast.

The first of these two night episodes is the trial of Jesus which ends with a judicial sentence leading to his death. The trial begins with false witnesses whose testimony, Mark stresses, does not agree. Indeed, deliberately or indeliberately, Mark has left their testimony about the destruction of the Temple incoherent for his readers; for he never explains what is false in the words they attribute to Jesus: "I will destroy this Temple that is made with hands, and in three days I will build another not made with hands." Did Jesus never say anything like this about the Temple? Or did he say something similar but not with the tone given by the witnesses? Did he prophesy destruction and restoration but not make himself the agent of the destruction (cf. John 2:19)? Or is the development of the tradition still more complicated, namely, that although the witnesses gave a false implication to Jesus' words, Mark is offering a clue for interpreting them correctly by the clarifying clauses "made with hands" and "not made with hands." This elegant pair of positive and negative Greek adjectives (found only in Mark) is very difficult to retrovert into Semitic; the adjectives, then, more likely represent a later Christian explanation that the Temple would be replaced by the Church.

In any case, the high priest is annoyed by both the ineptitude of the witnesses and the silence of Jesus—the silence which Christians found foretold in the Isaian picture of the Suffering Servant of the Lord (53:7). Seeking to force an answer, the high priest demands, "Are you the Messiah, the son of the Blessed?" God had proclaimed Jesus as His Son both at the baptism (Mark 1:11) and at the transfiguration (9:7); Peter had proclaimed Jesus as Messiah (8:29); and so it is not surprising that Jesus answers with an affirmative. But he then goes on to explain that he is not only the anointed Davidic prince expected to establish a kingdom: he is the Son of Man who at the endtime will come from God's presence to judge the world. His warning to the high priest, "You will see the Son of Man coming with the clouds of heaven," shows Jesus' conviction that even his enemies will be forced to recognize his triumph. The warning is rejected; the high priest sees only blasphemy in the claim that as Son of Man Jesus will sit at the right hand of the Power, and so he coerces *all* the judges to condemn Jesus as deserving death. Not a voice is raised in his defense. The malice of the procedure is further underlined when some of the Sanhedrin members spit on Jesus. Covering his face, they strike him, challenging him to prophesy. Once more, Christian readers would hear an echo of Isaiah's description of the Suffering Servant of the Lord (50:6): "I hid not my face from shame and spitting."

This trial has combined the themes of destroying the Temple and of acknowledging Jesus as Messiah/Son of God. These themes, which were already evident in the Marcan account of the public ministry, will recur twice more before the passion is over; and by the end Jesus' role as a prophet, mocked by the Sanhedrin, will be vindicated.

If Jesus has not yielded under questioning by the high priest, Peter's behavior under questioning by the retinue of the high priest is quite different. The Lord confesses; the disciple denies. Peter's first denial, directed to a maidservant, is a pretense not to understand, followed by an attempt to get away from the courtyard and from public attention. But the persistent maidservant pursues him, and so Peter is forced to deny his status as a disciple—he is not one of those associated with Jesus. A third denial intensifies the shame, for now Peter swears an oath that he does not even know Jesus. As Peter says this, he curses. If Mark means (as many scholars think) that he is cursing Jesus, truly Peter has reached the depths of degradation in his discipleship—many a later Christian reader of Mark would face martyrdom rather than deny or curse Jesus. But at this moment Peter remembers Jesus' prophetic words about a triple denial, and he is moved to weep. Thus Mark does not finish the portrait of Peter without a redeeming touch; after all, the same Jesus who had prophesied Peter's denials had included him in the promise: "After I am raised up, I will go before you to Galilee" (14:28). If one thinks again of future martyrs, the story of Peter could offer hope to those who had failed and denied Jesus. The reader in concluding this section should not miss the irony that at the very moment when Jesus is being mocked by the Sanhedrin challenge to prophesy, his prophecies are coming true.

C. ROMAN TRIAL (15:1-20)

Mark effects the transition from the Jewish trial to the Roman trial by a reference to a morning consultation of the whole Sanhedrin (15:1). It is not clear whether he intends to describe a second session of this body or is resumptively concluding the night session after the interruption effected by the account of Peter's denials. Nor does Mark make it clear why, when the Sanhedrin had condemned Jesus as deserving death, they do not execute the sentence but decide to bind him and deliver him to Pilate. (This logical difficulty is addressed only by John [18:31] among the evangelists.) It is almost as if Mark is telling a tale well-known and is not bothering to supply connectives; for when Pilate confronts Jesus, he has no need to be informed as to what has gone on or about the issues that were the subject of the Jewish trial. Nothing about the Temple or about the Messiah/Son of God is repeated. The issue is immediately shifted from the religious to the political: "Are you the King of the Jews?" (15:3)—a question about a title hitherto never used for Jesus by friend or foe, and therefore presumably reflecting the interests or fears of the Romans.

Jesus' ambiguous affirmation, "You have said so," is deemed no answer by Pilate (Mark 15:4), so that the motif of Jesus' silence before his captors, already echoed in the Jewish trial (14:61), reappears in the Roman trial. As the nations wondered at the Suffering Servant of the Lord who received no glory from others (Isa 52:15 Septuagint), so Pilate wonders at Jesus (Mark 15:5). In Mark's portrayal, the chief priests, having failed to move Pilate to condemn Jesus, are more successful with a crowd that has come to ask for the release of a prisoner on the feast. Knowing that the priests acted out of envious zeal, Pilate offers Jesus, the accused "King of the Jews," to this crowd; but the priests persuade them to ask instead for Barabbas, an imprisoned murderous rebel,[6] and to demand the crucifixion of Jesus. Pilate's last quoted words, "Why, what evil has he done?", serves to underline how outrageously Jesus is treated by those who might have been expected to be enthusiastic for their "King." The only thing that will satisfy them is the decision to flog and crucify Jesus.

Inevitably, there is an anti-Jewish tone in having the priests and, through them, the crowd so hostile to Jesus. Nevertheless, the Marcan portrayal of Pilate is less developed and less sympathetic than that of the other Gospels, and so the contrast with the Jewish leaders is less stark. In Mark, Pilate makes no intensive effort on Jesus'

[6] Certain manuscripts of Matthew will offer a peculiar insight into Barabbas; see p. 41 below.

Marcan Passion Narrative

behalf, and yields rather easily to the crowd in order to avoid unpopularity. The impression, then, is not one of the favorable Roman and the hostile Jew—rather it is of a Jesus who had no support on any side. That impression is reinforced by the gratuitous brutality of the Roman soldiers who interrupt the crucifixion process of flogging the criminal and leading him to the cross to vent their scorn on the "King of the Jews," striking him and spitting on him. Both trials end with mockery; the Jewish trial with the mocking of a prophet, the Roman trial with the mocking of a king. For neither Jew nor Roman was it enough that Jesus die; his claims had to be derided. In a sequence where Judas hands over Jesus to the chief priests (14:10-11), and the chief priests hand Jesus over to Pilate (15:1), and Pilate hands Jesus over to be crucified (15:15), it becomes clear that disciple, Jewish leader, and Roman leader all have a share of guilt.

D. CRUCIFIXION, DEATH, AND BURIAL (15:21-47)

Although among the four Gospels Mark provides the shortest account of the crucifixion, he makes every detail count. On the way to the cross, Mark pauses to identify Simon of Cyrene through the two sons Alexander and Rufus, perhaps because these men were known to the community for which Mark wrote. In his extremely laconic description of the act of crucifixion, Mark highlights the curious details of the offering of wine mixed with myrrh and the division of the garments—a sign of the influence of the Psalm passages 69:22; 22:19 that the later evangelists will make explicit.[7]

Mark's artistry is most apparent in his resort to an organizing pattern of threes (already used so effectively in Jesus' three-fold prayer at Gethsemane and in Peter's three

[7] See below pp. 43 and 64.

denials). Mark spells out a chronological pattern of the third, sixth, and ninth hours (9 A.M., noon, 3 P.M.). Between the third and the sixth hours, three groups mock the crucified. First, the reference to destroying and rebuilding the Temple is taken from the Jewish trial and hurled as a blasphemy at the crucified Jesus by chance passers-by who wag their heads and challenge him to save himself. Here Mark is echoing Psalm 22:8-9, a citation that Matthew will strengthen. Second, in a mounting crescendo the chief priests and the scribes take up another motif from the Jewish trial, mocking the pretension that Jesus is "the Messiah, the King of Israel." Third, even the criminals crucified with Jesus revile him.

If no human being shows Jesus sympathy in this first three-hour period, nature itself is plunged into a darkness that covers the whole land during the second, from the sixth to the ninth hour. Here Mark may be recalling the warning of Amos 8:9 that the sun would go down at noon and the light would be darkened on the earth by day.

Finally, at the ninth hour, Jesus cries out with a loud voice the only words that Mark reports. In response to three hours of mockery by all who spoke to him, and to three hours of nature's gloom, Jesus repeats the opening words of Psalm 22, asking, "My God, my God, why have you forsaken me?" This cry should not be softened,[8] any more than Jesus' plea to his Father in Gethsemane should be softened. It is paradoxical that the cry is quoted in Aramaic which carries the tone of the intimacy of Jesus' family language, and yet now for the first time Jesus speaks to Yahweh as "God," instead of as "Father." Mark is brutally realistic in showing that, while this desperate plea causes some to offer Jesus wine, it leads to skeptical

[8] Under the Matthean form of this cry I shall discuss the implicit christology involved.

Marcan Passion Narrative

mockery by others whose cynicism about Elijah's help constitutes the last human words that Jesus will hear—and no Elijah comes to deliver him. John the Baptist had come in the Elijah role not to deliver Jesus, but to die a martyr's death and point to the type of violent death that awaits Jesus (9:12-13). In the Marcan account of the ministry, the demons had cried out with a loud voice as they encountered the presence of God's Son. In this hour of darkness, as Jesus struggles with Satan, it is God's Son who cries out a second time with a loud voice as he expires. The apocalyptic scene evokes the words of Joel 2:10-11; 4:16: "The sun and moon shall be darkened . . . and the Lord shall give His voice before His host. . . . The Lord will give His voice from Jerusalem and the heavens and the earth will be shaken, but the Lord will spare His people."

The Lord God's response to His Son's cry is described with stunning abruptness by Mark. The moment Jesus expires the curtain of the Temple is torn in two from top to bottom. Scholars debate whether the veil was the one that separated the outer court from the sanctuary or the inner veil that led to the Holy of Holies—a debate often centered on the symbolic signs attached to each veil. There is nothing, however, to suggest that Mark's readers (or even Mark himself) would have had the specialized knowledge to understand the difference or the symbolism. More important is the debate whether the tearing of the Temple veil is meant to signify the displeasure of God abandoning the Temple or an opening of a once-closed sacred place to a wider audience, especially to the Gentiles. While the latter allows a more benevolent interpretation of Mark's attitude toward Judaism, the former is more probable, even if more unpleasant. The language of "schism" from top to bottom indicates a violent rending, similar to the high priest's tearing his garments in judgment at the trial of Jesus.

Indeed, that trial supplies two motifs that recur here immediately after Jesus' death—motifs repeated already once in the mockery at the foot of the cross. The rending of the Temple veil is the incipient fulfillment of the saying attributed to Jesus at the trial: "I will destroy this Temple that is made with hands." With the veil torn, this Temple is being destroyed, not being opened to outsiders; for the Temple to which the outsiders will come is one not built with hands. And the first of the outsiders comes immediately. Seeing how Jesus expired, a Roman centurion confesses, "Truly this man was Son of God." He thus evokes the second motif from the Jewish trial where Jesus was adjured to state whether he was "the Messiah, the Son of the Blessed One." Jesus' answers at the trial caused him to be mocked as a false prophet, but now the prophet is verified. Not only is the Temple being destroyed, but also for the first time in the Gospel a human being has recognized Jesus' identity as God's Son.

Abandoned by his disciples, betrayed by Judas, denied by Peter, accused of blasphemy by the priests, rejected in favor of a murderer by the crowd, mocked by the Sanhedrin and by Roman troops and by all who came to the cross, surrounded by darkness, and seemingly forsaken by his God, in this one dramatic moment Jesus is fully vindicated. God has answered Jesus' cry by replacing the Temple as the locus of worship and by offering in its place His own Son who will be confessed by Gentile and Jew alike. Only after the centurion's confession are we told that some of Jesus' followers, women who had ministered to him, and others from Galilee, were at Golgotha; and we are led to assume that they too would have shared the centurion's confession. Mark is specific about the reaction of one Jewish figure, Joseph of Arimathea, "a respected member of the Sanhedrin." He had been "looking for the Kingdom of God," but Jesus' death brought him forward to ask for the body of the crucified. Only Mark stresses that this was an act of courage— understandably, since Mark has told us that *all* the members of the Sanhedrin had found Jesus deserving of death.

The Roman centurion and Joseph of Arimathea dramatize Mark's theological outlook on the importance of the passion. People can believe and become true disciples only through the suffering symbolized by a cross which strips away human supports and makes one totally dependent on God. Jesus had been taunted to come down from the cross and save himself, whereas salvation comes only through the acceptance of the cross. If the crucifixion of Jesus is described by Mark with greater severity and starkness than is found in the other Gospels, perhaps the Marcan message had to encourage a community that had endured a particularly severe testing. (The ancient tradition that Mark was addressed to Roman Christians would make sense if they had seen "a vast multitude" brutally martyred under Nero.) The gospel or "Good News" for them was that this trial and suffering was not a defeat but a salvific example of taking up the cross and following Jesus.

At the close of the passion narrative, only Mark among the Synoptics tells us that Pilate checked whether Jesus was dead. This emphasis may be a sign that already Christian apologists were wrestling with the claim that Jesus, not really dead, had been revived by the chill of the tomb, a charge that would be given new emphasis by 18th and 19th century rationalists! Mark's double stress on the presence of Mary Magdalene and the other women (15:40, 47) who "saw where Jesus was laid" is meant to prepare for their Sunday morning visit to a tomb that would be found empty. For Mark, the story of Jesus' death does not close with his burial, but with his resurrection.

Marcan Passion Narrative

The Passion According to Matthew

The same liturgical year (A) that offers the Matthean passion account on Palm/Passion Sunday draws from the rest of Matthew on the Sundays of the Ordinary Time. Once again this reminds us to set the passion in the context of the whole Gospel story. For instance Matthew opens with Herod the king, the chief priests, and the scribes seeking the death of the child Jesus;[9] as Matthew comes to an end Pilate the governor, the chief priests, and the scribes are instrumental in putting Jesus to death. The two scenes contain Matthew's only references to Jesus as "the King of the Jews." In the infancy narrative there is a five-fold pattern of scenes alternating between those friendly to Jesus (Mary, Joseph, magi) and those hostile to him (Herod, chief priests, scribes). In the burial narrative there is a similar fivefold pattern of alternating friends (Joseph of Arimathea, Mary Magdalene, women, disciples) and enemies (chief priests, Pharisees, guards).[10] Deeper meaning is found in some of those who appear in the passion if we remember their role in the ministry. The Matthean disciples (unlike the Marcan disciples) have clearly professed that Jesus is the Son of God (14:33), and so their failure and flight from Gethsemane is all the more shocking. The Matthean Peter, rescued by Jesus from sinking in the sea (14:30-31), has spoken for all in confessing Jesus as "the Messiah, the Son of the living God"; this makes truly poignant his repeated denial, "I do not know the man" (27:72, 74). In Matthew (23:1-36) Jesus' critique of the

[9] Matthew 2:5, 16, 20 ("those who have sought the child's life").
[10] Compare 1:18–2:23 to 27:57–28:20.

Matthean Passion Narrative

Pharisees is particularly severe. Yet, while Matthew (27:62) mentions the Pharisees among the adversaries of Jesus during the passion, he does so only once (elsewhere only John 18:3) and so supports the general Gospel contention that the (Sadducee) chief priests were the principal Jewish agents in Jesus' death. If the Gentile magi are set over against Jewish figures hostile to the child Jesus at the beginning of Matthew's Gospel, the Gentile wife of Pilate is a similar contrasting figure in the trial of Jesus; and both function in a uniquely Matthean context of revelation given in dreams. The dire self-condemnatory "His blood on us and on our children" (27:25) has an antecedent in the self-condemnation of the chief priests and the elders in 21:41 who interpret the parable of the vineyard to mean: "He [God] will put those wretches to a miserable death and let out the vineyard to other tenants." It has a sequence in that by the end of the Gospel (28:15) "the Jews" are an alien group to the followers of Jesus.

But let us move on from the overall context of the Gospel to the individual scenes of the Matthean passion account. Because of the closeness of Matthew to Mark in the passion (p. 20 above), I shall not repeat elements in the previous chapter that are also applicable to Matthew.

A. GETHSEMANE: PRAYER AND ARREST (26:30-56)

The echoes of the Last Supper die out with the hymn the disciples sing as they go to the Mount of Olives, perhaps a hymn of the Passover liturgy. This Mount is mentioned twice in the OT. In Zechariah 14:4ff. it is the site to which God will come from heaven to judge the world—a reference that explains why Luke specifies the Mount of Olives as the place of Jesus' ascension and ultimate return (Acts 1:9-12). More important for our purposes, in II Samuel 15:30-31 David in peril of his life has to flee Jerusalem from Absalom's revolt; he goes to the Mount of

Olives and weeps there, discovering that he has been
betrayed by Ahitophel, his trusted advisor. Small wonder
that in Matthew this Mount is the site where Jesus
predicts desertion by his disciples, denial by Peter, and
where he is arrested through the treason of Judas. The
story of the Davidic Messiah echoes the story of David;
and yet the attachment of the arrest to Gethsemane, "oil
press," an otherwise unknown locale on the Mount, sug-
gests a basis in historical tradition, rather than pure symbolism.

Before Judas arrives at Gethsemane, the relation between Jesus and his disciples comes to a dramatic finale.
Leaving behind the group of the disciples and then the
three chosen ones, Jesus goes on alone to pray, falling on
his face to the earth, with his soul sorrowful like that of
the Psalmist (Ps 42:6—another instance of the all-
pervasive OT coloring of the Passion Narrative).[11] The
touching prayer he pours forth in this moment of distress
has often been the subject of historical skepticism. The
disciples were at a distance and asleep; how could anyone
know what Jesus said to God? It may be observed,
however, that the words Matthew attributes to Jesus in
Gethsemane echo the Lord's Prayer: "My Father"; "Pray
that you may not enter into temptation"; "Your will be
done." We know of a tradition that Jesus prayed when he
faced death, for in Hebrews 5:7 we read, "Christ offered
prayers and supplications with cries and tears to God who
was able to save him from death." It is not implausible
that Christian reflection filled in this prayer with words
patterned on Jesus' prayer during his ministry. This would
have been a way of affirming that Jesus' relationship to
his Father remained consistent through life and death.

[11] For the christological tension between the situation in Gethsemane and
Jesus' prophetic confidence during the ministry, see my discussion of the Marcan
account above.

Matthean Passion Narrative

36

The three times Jesus withdraws to pray and the three times he returns to find the disciples sleeping exemplify the well-attested literary pattern of "the three," namely, that stories are effective and balanced if three characters or three incidents are included. The repetition underlines the continued obtuseness of the disciples and makes their inability to keep awake a perceptive comment on Jesus' prayer that the cup pass from him. It will not pass, and in his moment of trial he will not be assisted by his disciples. Yet Jesus' prayer is not without effect: it begins with him sorrowful, troubled, and prostrate; it ends with him on his feet resolutely facing the hour that has approached: "Rise, let us be going; see, my betrayer is at hand."

The betrayer is "Judas, one of the Twelve." The identification of Judas at this point, as if he had never been mentioned before, is often hailed as a sign that the Passion Narrative was once an independent unit that needed to introduce the dramatis personae. But "one of the Twelve," as it now stands in Matthew 26, a chapter that has already twice mentioned Judas, helps to catch the heinousness of a betrayal by one who had been an intimate. This intimacy is further stressed when Jesus addresses him as "Friend" or "Companion," a touch peculiar to Matthew here (and previously used as a disappointed address to one who should have been grateful in 20:13). Also Matthean is Jesus' rebuke of armed resistance: "Put your sword back in place, for all who take up the sword will perish by it." There are traces in the Gospels of Christian puzzlement that, when Jesus was arrested, a sword was raised. This puzzlement surely increased when the identification of the assailant moved from Mark's vague "bystander" to "one of the followers of Jesus" (Matthew) to "Simon Peter" (John); and so the later Gospels must clarify that such action was not directed by Jesus. On the other hand, the helplessness of Jesus against those who arrested him was also a problem since the tradition reported previous occasions when he had frustrated attempts to seize him. Matthew has Jesus giving an assurance: "Do you think that I cannot appeal to my Father, and he will at once send me more than twelve legions of angels?" The ultimate explanation is that Jesus is allowing such indignities so that "the prophetic Scriptures might be fulfilled."

B. SANHEDRIN TRIAL; PETER'S DENIAL AND JUDAS' DESPERATION (26:57–27:10)

Matthew is alone among the Synoptics in identifying as "Caiaphas" the high priest before whom Jesus was brought for trial after being arrested. No part of the passion narrative has been more disputed historically than the trial of Jesus before the Jewish Sanhedrin. A session in the middle of the night on a major Jewish feast where the high priest encourages false witness and then intervenes to tell the judges that the prisoner is guilty, and where the judges themselves spit on the prisoner and slap him—all of that violates jurisprudence in general and rabbinic jurisprudence in particular. Moreover, it is never made clear why, having sentenced the prisoner as liable to death, the Sanhedrin then handed him over to the Roman governor for a new trial. (The explanation that the Sanhedrin did not have the right of capital punishment comes from John and does not help us with Matthew.) There are, of course, possible explanations, but these should not distract us from the impression Matthew wants to give. His evangelical concern is to convince his readers that Jesus was totally innocent, for the blasphemy charged against him had distorted his words and intent. Yet there is also irony. Despite the falsehood in the anti-Temple words attributed to Jesus, Matthew's readers in the 80s know that the Temple really was destroyed; and they are invited to see this as a sign of retribution. Despite the malice of the high

Matthean Passion Narrative

priest, they also know that Jesus' answer to the definitive question was true: he is the Son of God and is seated at the right hand of the power. If the portrait of the Sanhedrin is unrelievedly hostile, we must remember that Matthew is writing to Christians who themselves have suffered from confrontations with synagogue leaders. We cannot impose our different religious sensibilities on the first century (see p. 15 above).

The president and the members of the Sanhedrin are not the only ones set over against Jesus in this drama. At the very moment Jesus is being interrogated by the Jewish court, Peter is being interrogated in the courtyard below by maids and bystanders—again the effective pattern of three times. Jesus shows himself resolute, remaining silent before false witnesses and nuancing his answer to the high priest; but Peter tries to avoid the issue ("I do not know what you mean"); then he lies ("I do not know the man"); and finally he abjures Jesus with an oath.[12] The best proof that Jesus' words before the Sanhedrin will ultimately come true is offered by the fact that, even as he utters them, his previous prediction about Peter is being verified: "Before the cock crows, you will deny me three times."

Indeed, still another prophecy of Jesus is verified as he is taken to be delivered to Pilate. Among the evangelists, only Matthew stops at this moment to dramatize a threatening word that Jesus had spoken to another of his followers earlier in the night: "Woe to that man by whom the Son of Man is betrayed; it would be better for him if he had never been born" (26:24). Logically Matthew's reintroduction of Judas here is awkward. The chief priests and elders are said to lead Jesus to Pilate (27:1); yet simul-

---

[12] No less than in Mark (above), Matthew's account of Peter's denials, followed implicitly by a rehabilitation so that he became a rock of Christian faith, could have served to encourage those who failed when first tested by persecution.

Matthean Passion Narrative

39

taneously they are portrayed in the Temple wrestling with the issue of the blood money that Judas has thrown back. They decide to buy with the money a burial field for Judas who has hanged himself (even as did Ahitophel who, as we saw, betrayed David: II Sam 17:23). This detail increases the awkwardness of the Matthean narrative if one thinks of Acts 1:18-19 where Judas himself buys the field and dies from a type of internal combustion (even as did the anti-God figure Antiochus Epiphanes in II Macc 9:7-10). We must assume that, unexpectedly, Judas died soon after the crucifixion and that early Christians connected the "Field of Blood" where he was buried with his betrayal or his death, a death described according to patterns supplied by the demises of OT unworthies.

However, the main goal of Matthew's narrative about Judas is in a different direction. Judas' violent death matches Jesus' prophecy, and the use of his ill-gotten thirty pieces of silver matches prophecies of Jeremiah and Zechariah. A divinely sketched triptych has provided not only Jesus on trial in the center panel, but also Peter's denial on one side-panel and Judas' desperation on the other. The mystery of the different fate of these two prominent disciples, both of whom failed Jesus, is penetratingly captured by Matthew's laconic description of the last action taken by each in the passion narrative: Peter "went out and wept bitterly"; Judas "went away and hanged himself."

c. ROMAN TRIAL (27:11-31)

Deserted by disciples, surrounded by enemies, Jesus now confronts the governor who can decree his death. Self-possessed, Jesus remains silent—a silence that puts the governor on the defensive. Matthew joins the other evangelists in describing the custom of releasing a prisoner at the feast, a custom that provides a possible solution for Pilate. Yet, despite the fourfold reference of the Gospels to

Matthean Passion Narrative

Barabbas, this episode has been the subject of much scholarly controversy, for such an amnesty custom is not attested among either the Romans or the Jews. (The parallels offered by ingenious defenders of historicity leave much to be desired when examined carefully.) Matthew's account is the most problematical because it is interrupted by the dream of Pilate's wife. As a dramatic touch, however, this peculiarly Matthean insert is highly effective: a Gentile woman through dream-revelation recognizes Jesus' innocence and seeks his release, while the Jewish leaders work through the crowd to have the notorious Barabbas released and Jesus crucified. Some important manuscripts of Matthew's Gospel counterpose Barabbas and Jesus in a unique way, for they phrase Pilate's question in 26:17 thus: "Whom do you want me to release to you—Jesus Barabbas or Jesus called Christ?" Since "Barabbas" probably means "Son of the Father," it is a fascinating irony to think that Pilate may have faced two men charged with a crime, both named Jesus, one "Son of the Father," the other "Son of God." But Matthew calls no attention to the meaning of the patronymic; he is satisfied with the irony of the guilty man being acclaimed and the innocent being thrust toward death.

The governor is overwhelmed by the demand of all for the crucifixion of Jesus; and so, in a dramatic gesture peculiar to Matthew's account, he publicly washes his hands to signify, "I am innocent of this [just] man's blood." Like his wife, the Gentile recognizes innocence; but "all the people" answer: "His blood on us and on our children." No line in the passion narratives has done more to embitter Jewish and Christian relations than this. It echoes OT language describing those who must be considered responsible for death (II Sam 3:28-29; Josh 2:19; Jer 26:15), even as washing one's hands is an OT action signifying innocence in reference to murder (Deut 21:6-9).

Matthean Passion Narrative

One can benevolently reflect that the Matthean statement was not applicable to the whole Jewish people of Jesus' time, for relatively few stood before Pilate, and also that it was an affirmation of present willingness to accept responsibility, not an invocation of future punishment or vengeance. (Yet rabbinic law exemplified in Mishnah *Sanhedrin* 4:5 holds perjurers accountable for the blood of an innocent man until the end of time.) On the whole Matthew's attitude is generalizing and hostile, and we cannot disguise it.[13] He thinks of the Pharisees and Sadducees as a "brood of vipers" who kill and crucify saintly prophets, wise men, and scribes, so that on them comes "all the righteous blood shed on earth, beginning with the blood of the innocent Abel" (23:33-35). Judas acknowledged that he had sinned in betraying Jesus' innocent blood; Pilate dramatized his own innocence of this just man's blood; but "all the people" agree that, if Jesus is innocent, his blood will be on them and their children. Any amelioration of this self-judgment in Matthew must be sought in the words that Jesus spoke at the supper, referring to his blood "as poured out for many [all] for the forgiveness of sins" (26:27).

The obduracy of the leaders and the people leads Pilate to have Jesus flogged and crucified. Ultimately, then, the Roman governor passes on Jesus the same sentence that the Jewish high priest passed; and at the end of the Roman trial Jesus is mocked and spat upon and struck even as he was at the end of the Jewish trial. Matthew has shown Pilate and his wife as favorable to Jesus, but the Galilean is a challenge to Gentiles as well as to Jews and is rejected by many from both sides.

---

[13] For the obligation to deal pastorally with such passages lest they produce anti-Semitism, see pp. 15–16 above.

Matthean Passion Narrative

D. CRUCIFIXION, DEATH, AND BURIAL (27:32-66)

The journey to Golgotha, which introduces Simon of Cyrene, is narrated with almost disconcerting brevity, as Matthew hews close to Mark in the finale of the story. Incidents at the place of execution are merely listed with little comment and no pathos. If there is a dominating motif behind the selection, it is correspondence to the OT. For instance, only Matthew has Jesus offered wine mixed with gall—an echo of Psalm 69:22: "For my food you gave me gall, and for my thirst sour wine to drink."

As in Mark, three groups parade by the cross in derision of Jesus. (Once more the pattern of "the three.") The most general group of passers-by begins by blaspheming against Jesus' claim to destroy the Temple, echoing the false witnesses of the trial. Also choosing a motif from the trial, the chief priests with the scribes and elders mock Jesus' claim to be Son of God. Without specification the robbers are said to revile in a similar manner. Peculiarly Matthean is the phrasing of the mockery so as to strengthen the reference to Psalm 22:8-9: "All who see me scoff at me; they deride me . . . . 'He trusted in the Lord; let Him deliver him.'"

Darkness covers the land at the sixth hour (noon) until the ninth hour (3 P.M.) when Jesus finally breaks his silence with a loud cry, making his only and final statement: "*Eli, Eli, lema sabachthani;* my God, my God, why have you forsaken me?" Matthew's Semitic form of the first verse of Psalm 22 is more Hebraized than Mark's "*Eloi, Eloi, lama sabachthani*" and makes more intelligible the misunderstanding by the bystanders that Jesus is calling for Elijah. Those who exalt the divinity of Jesus to the point where they cannot allow him to be truly human interpret away this verse to fit their christology. They insist that Psalm 22 ends with God delivering the suffering figure. That may well be, but the verse that Jesus is por-

Matthean Passion Narrative

trayed as quoting is not the verse of deliverance but the verse of abandonment—a verse by a suffering psalmist who is puzzled because up to now God has always supported and heard him. It is an exaggeration to speak of Jesus' despair, for he still speaks to "*my* God." Yet Matthew, following Mark, does not hesitate to show Jesus in the utter agony of feeling forsaken as he faces a terrible death. We are not far here from the christology of Hebrews which portrays Jesus as experiencing the whole human condition, like us in everything except sin. Only if we take these words seriously can we see the logic of the Matthean Jesus' anguished prayer that this cup might pass from him.

In Matthew's view God has not forsaken Jesus, and that becomes obvious immediately after his death. All three Synoptics know of the tearing of the Temple curtain, but only Matthew reports an earthquake where rocks are split and tombs are opened and the dead rise. Some of these phenomena resemble wondrous events that the Jewish historian Josephus associates with the destruction of Jerusalem and the Temple by the Romans under Titus. Certainly, too, there are echoes of OT apocalyptic passages (Joel 2:10; Ezek 37:12; Isa 26:19; Nahum 1:5-6; Dan 12:2). Matthew did not hesitate to have the moment of Jesus' birth marked by a star in the sky; the moment of his death is even more climactic, marked by signs in the heavens, on the earth, and under the earth. It is a moment of judgment on a Judaism represented by the Temple; a moment of new life for the saintly dead of Israel; and a moment of opportunity for the Gentiles, represented by the Roman guards who confess, "Truly this man was the Son of God."

What follows is anticlimactic. Matthew, like Mark, mentions the women followers of Jesus but does nothing to relate their "looking on from a distance" to the stupendous phenomena they should have seen. The tradition of Joseph of Arimathea, common to all four Gospels, is embellished in Matthew. Joseph is "a rich man," probably a deduction from his owning a tomb, but also a sign that for Matthew's community the model of a rich saint is not repugnant. He is also a disciple of Jesus, and the tomb in which Jesus is buried is *his*. These details, missing from Mark, complicate the scene. If a disciple buried Jesus, why can Jesus' women followers only look on without participating? Does Matthew's tradition represent a simplified remembrance about a pious Jew who buried Jesus in loyalty to Deut 21:22-23, which stipulates that the body of a criminal should not hang overnight? Did this Jew subsequently become a believer in Jesus, whence the tradition that he was a disciple?

Entirely peculiar to Matthew is the aftermath of the burial where the chief priests and Pharisees get permission from Pilate to post a guard at the tomb. These soldiers were meant to frustrate any machinations based on Jesus' prediction that he would rise on the third day; but, as Matthew sees it, their presence helped to confirm the resurrection since it excluded obvious natural explanations as to why the tomb was empty. For good reasons most scholars are skeptical about the historicity of this scene in Matthew. Elsewhere the followers of Jesus are portrayed as showing no expectation that Jesus would rise, and so it is unlikely that the chief priests and Pharisees would anticipate this. Moreover, no other evangelist shows any awareness that the women coming to the tomb on Easter morning would face an armed guard. Matthew's story fits into his apologetics as we see from its conclusion. In the last words they speak in this Gospel the chief priests tell the soldiers to lie, and that lie "has been spread among the Jews to this day" (28:15). By the time this Gospel is written, the synagogue and the church are accusing each other of deceit about the principal Christian claim. More theologically, the guard at the tomb helps Matthew to illustrate the awesome power of God associated with Jesus. Men do all they can to make certain that Jesus is finished and his memory is buried; they even seal and guard his tomb. Yet the God who shook the earth when Jesus died will shake it again on Sunday morning; the guards will grovel in fear (28:2-4); and the tomb will be opened to stand as an eloquent witness that God has verified the last promise made by His Son: Jesus sits at the right hand of the Power (26:64).

The Passion According to Luke

In the C or third year of the liturgical cycle, the Lucan passion narrative is read on Palm/Passion Sunday, even as its Synoptic "brethren," Matthew and Mark, have been read in A and B years, and before the Johannine passion is read on Good Friday. This "in-between" setting is appropriate, for in many aspects of the passion Luke stands between Mark/Matthew and John. Nowhere else, when there is common material, does Luke so differ from Mark—a fact that has prompted a debate whether Luke drew on a consecutive passion narrative other than Mark. In many of the differences from Mark, both factual and theological, Luke approaches John. Yet once again neither technical inter-Gospel comparisons nor corresponding historical issues are a major concern in this short book which concentrates on material for Holy Week reflection.

The Lucan passion narrative is read in the same liturgical year in which the Gospel of Luke has supplied the readings on the Sundays of the Ordinary Time; it will be followed immediately in the Easter Season by readings from the Acts of the Apostles, the other half of the Lucan two-volume work. This total setting is necessary to understand the passion message, for the original author (conventionally but very uncertainly identified as Luke, the companion of Paul) is a consistent thinker and writer. The Jesus who is accused before Pilate by the chief priests and scribes of "perverting our nation" (Luke 23:2) is one whose infancy and upbringing was totally in fidelity to the Law of Moses (2:22, 27, 39, 42). Similarly, the Jesus who is accused of "forbidding us to give tribute to Caesar" is a Jesus who had only recently (20:25) declared concerning the tribute: "Render to Caesar the things that are Caesar's." All of this casts light on the affirmation made by various dramatis personae in the passion that Jesus is innocent (23:4, 14, 22, 41, 47). The Jesus who calmly faces death is one who had already set his face deliberately to go to Jerusalem (9:51), affirming that no prophet should perish away from Jerusalem (13:33). In the Lucan account of the ministry Jesus showed tenderness to the stranger (the widow of Nain) and praised the mercy shown to the Prodigal Son and to the man beset by thieves on the road to Jericho; it is not surprising then that in his passion Jesus shows forgiveness to those who crucified him. When one has been forewarned that the devil departed from Jesus after the temptations "until the opportune time" (4:13), one is not surprised to find the devil returning in this hour of the passion which belongs to "the power of darkness" (22:53) and entering into Judas the betrayer (22:3), while demanding to sift Simon Peter the denier (22:31).

Luke, who has described the disciples/apostles with extraordinary delicacy during the ministry (unlike Mark who dwells on their failures and weaknesses), continues a merciful portrayal of them during the passion, never mentioning that they fled. Indeed, he places male acquaintances of Jesus at Calvary (23:49). This fits with Luke's unique post-resurrectional picture where all the appearances of Jesus are in the Jerusalem area (as if the disciples had never fled back to Galilee), and where apostles like Peter and John will become chief actors in the Book of Acts. The Jesus of the passion, accused by chief priests before the Roman governor and the Herodian king, prepares the way for a Paul brought before the same cast of adversaries (Acts 21:27-25:27). The innocent Jesus who dies asking forgiveness for his enemies and commending his soul to God the Father prepares the way for the first Christian martyr,

Stephen, who will perish uttering similar sentiments (Acts 7:59-60). Consistency from the Law and the Prophets to Jesus and ultimately to the Church is a Lucan theme in which the passion is a major component.

A. MOUNT OF OLIVES:
PRAYER AND ARREST (22:39-53)

The Lucan form of this scene[14] is less suspenseful and dramatic in relation to the disciples than is the comparable account in Mark/Matthew. Jesus goes to a *customary place*, the Mount of Olives,[15] so that Judas has no problem in finding him. No words of rebuke are spoken to the disciples who follow Jesus. After all, at the Last Supper (in Luke alone) Jesus has praised them by anticipation, "You are those who have continued with me in my trials"; and he has assured them that they will have a kingdom, as well as a place at the eschatological table, and thrones of judgment (22:28, 29)—how can they then seriously fall away? Accordingly, Jesus does not separate himself from the body of the disciples and then from the three chosen ones, as he does in Mark/Matthew. He simply withdraws a stone's throw urging them to pray. If they sleep, it is "for sorrow" (22:45); and they are found sleeping only once, not three times.

All the drama in the scene is centered in Luke's unique portrayal of Jesus. He is not one whose soul is sorrowful unto death or who lies prostrate in the dust. He has prayed often during the ministry; so now on his knees he

[14] Even though, for reasons of manageability and intelligibility, under the rubric "passion" I continue to confine the discussion to the sequence of events from *Gethsemane to the grave*, this procedure may be least justifiable in the case of Luke; for the whole of chapter 22, including the Last Supper, is clearly united with the passion in the author's design (see pp. 19–20 above).

[15] Luke, writing for Gentiles, avoids what to them might be unintelligible Semitisms, like Gethsemane and Golgotha.

utters a prayer to his Father prefaced and concluded by a subordination of his will to God's wish. The Son's prayer does not remain unanswered; rather God sends an angel to strengthen him.[16] This divine assistance brings Jesus to *agōnia* (whence the "agony" in the garden), a Greek term which does not refer to agony in the ordinary sense but describes the supreme tension of the athlete covered with sweat at the start of the contest. In that spirit Jesus rises from his prayer ready to enter the trial, even as he mercifully tells his disciples to pray that they be spared from that trial (22:46).

It is a mark of exquisite Lucan sensitivity that when the arresting party comes, led by Judas, the perverse kiss is forestalled. Jesus addresses his betrayer by name (the only time in all the Gospels) and shows a foreknowledge of the planned strategy (22:48). Sensitively, too, Luke adds a motif to the traditional cutting off the ear of the high priest's slave, namely, that Jesus who has so often healed in the ministry heals this opponent, even in the midst of his own peril. The figures who come to arrest Jesus on the Mount of Olives are not simply emissaries of the Jewish authorities as in the other Gospels; rather, the high priests, the Temple officers, and the elders themselves come out against him. The scene of the arrest terminates with Jesus' dramatic announcement that it is their hour; with them the power of darkness has come (22:53).

B. PETER'S DENIAL; SANHEDRIN INTERROGATION (22:54-71)

As Jesus is arrested, he is taken to the high priest's house; but seemingly no judicial procedure occurs until day comes (22:66). The night activity is centered on the court-

---

[16] The Lucan passion narrative has key verses that are textually dubious, 22:43-44; 23:34. I agree with the increasing number of scholars who regard these as genuine Lucan texts, omitted by later scribes for theological reasons.

yard. There, after three denials, what causes Peter to weep bitterly is not simply the remembrance of Jesus' prediction; it is the look given to him by Jesus who seemingly is present all the time that Peter is denying him! This dramatic look, peculiar to Luke, is an aspect of Jesus' continuing care for Peter promised at the Last Supper (22:32). The courtyard is also the scene of the abuse of Jesus as a prophet, an action which ironically confirms his foreknowledge that he would die in Jerusalem as a prophet (13:33).

After the denials and the mockery of the night, when day has come, Jesus is led away to the Sanhedrin by the elders, the scribes, and the chief priests (presumably the priests Annas and Caiaphas mentioned so prominently by Luke at the beginning of the public ministry in 3:2). This collective leadership, and not a single high priest as in the other Gospels, poses to Jesus a series of separate questions about his identity as the Messiah and as the Son of God. Jesus answers these questions ambiguously (even as he does during the ministry in John 10:22-39); he will die a martyr's death, but he does not foolishly force the hands of his captors. There are no witnesses and no condemnation at this Sanhedrin session, so that one gets the impression of an interrogation preparatory to the one and only trial conducted by the Roman governor—an impression quite unlike that given by Mark/Matthew. One must not assume, however, that Luke does not hold the Jewish authorities responsible for the execution of Jesus, for numerous passages in Acts affirm such responsibility (see p. 14 above). The self-composure of Jesus throughout the sequence of Peter's denials, the mockery, and the questions is striking. It is not the majestic supremacy of the Johannine Jesus, but the God-given tranquillity of one to whom the Father has delivered all things (Luke 10:22) and the human tranquillity of one who is totally innocent.

Lucan Passion Narrative

C. THE TRIAL BEFORE PILATE AND HEROD (23:1-25)

Luke's staging of the Roman trial, almost as elaborate as John's, goes considerably beyond the picture in Mark/Matthew. Although some of the same basic material is included (the issue of the "King of the Jews" and the alternative offered by Barabbas), the overall development is uniquely shaped by parallelism with the Roman trials of Paul in Acts 16:19-24; 17:6-9; 18:12-17; 23:23-30. There are clear similarities in such features as detailed charges involving violations of Roman law and of Caesar's majesty, an indifference by Roman officials to the religious issues that are really involved, and the desire to let the prisoner go, or at most chastise him with a whipping.

The unique and fascinating Lucan contribution to the Pilate scene is the interspersed trial before Herod, the tetrarch or "king" of Galilee, who is present in Jerusalem for the feast, and to whom Pilate sends Jesus upon learning that he is a Galilean. Christian memory has preserved a series of Herodian adversary images: a Herod (the Great) who with the chief priests and scribes conspired to kill the child Jesus (Matt 2); a Herod (Antipas) who killed John the Baptist (Mark 6:17-29; Matt 14:3-12), reputedly sought to kill Jesus (Luke 13:31), and would be remembered as aligned with Pilate against Jesus (Acts 4:27); a Herod (Agrippa I) who killed James, son of Zebedee, and sought to kill Peter (Acts 12:1-5); and a Herod (Agrippa II) who sat in judgment on Paul alongside a Roman governor (Acts 25:13-27). These traditions have been woven together into the passion narrative in different ways in the apocryphal *Gospel of Peter* (where Herod becomes Jesus' chief adversary who crucifies him) and in Luke. Although annoyed by Jesus' silence, and contemptuously mocking him—two details that the other Gospels relate to Jesus' appearance before Pilate—the Lucan Herod confirms Pilate's judgment that Jesus is innocent (Luke

Lucan Passion Narrative

23:14-15). In turn, contact with Jesus heals the enmity that had existed between the Galilean "king" and the Roman, an enmity that may have been caused by Pilate's brutally killing Galileans (Luke 13:1). Once more Jesus has a healing effect even on those who maltreat him.

D. CRUCIFIXION, DEATH, AND BURIAL (23:26-56)

In this section of the passion narrative, Luke is most individualistic. Since he narrates no mocking of Jesus by Roman soldiers after Pilate's sentence, the deliverance of Jesus "up to their will" (23:25) creates the impression that the ones who seize Jesus, take him to Calvary, and crucify him are the chief priests, the Jewish rulers, and the people—the last plural subject mentioned (23:13). Eventually, however, we hear of soldiers (23:36), presumably Roman; and the people are shown as following Jesus, without hostility, lamenting. Thus Luke alone among the passion narrators portrays a segment of Jews who are not disciples of Jesus but who are touched by his suffering and death. Jesus addresses these "daughters of Jerusalem," not in reference to his own impending fate, but to the catastrophe that awaits them. They belong to a city that has killed the prophets and refused all Jesus' overtures of grace, a city already destined to be dashed to the ground and trodden by Gentiles (13:34-35; 19:41-44; 21:20-24). Elsewhere, Luke shows great reluctance in having Jesus speak harshly; if he permits that here in threatening words borrowed from Isaiah (54:1-4) and Hosea (10:8), Luke is probably constrained by the factuality of the destruction of Jerusalem that has already taken place at Roman hands by the time he writes.

The contrast in Jesus' attitudes is heightened by the first words he speaks upon coming to the place of the Skull: "Father, forgive them for they know not what they do."[17]

[17] See footnote 16 above.

This hint that the Jewish chief priests and scribes acted out of ignorance, which is reiterated in Acts (3:17), runs against the general NT judgment of deliberate blindness and malevolence on the part of the Jewish authorities involved in the crucifixion. It constitutes not only a more humane understanding of the complex responsibilities for the death of Jesus (pp. 13–16 above), but also a directive for the gracious treatment of one's enemies that has often been simply called "Christian." There are many who would come after Jesus, beginning with Stephen (Acts 7:60), who would find hope in facing unjust brutality by repeating the prayer of the Lucan Jesus.

Three groups (but not the people) mock the crucified Jesus in response to his forgiving words: the rulers, the soldiers, and *one* of the two criminals crucified with him. In a major departure from the Synoptic tradition, the other criminal in Luke acknowledges the justice of his own sentence and confesses the innocence of one whom he addresses intimately as "Jesus"—an address used elsewhere in the Gospels in a friendly manner only by the blind beggar of Jericho. And the suffering Jesus responds with greater generosity than the petitioner requests, for Jesus will not simply remember the man after entering into his Kingdom;[18] he will take the man with him this very day. The oft-used observation that the "good thief" ultimately stole the Kingdom is not too far from the truth.

In the last hours of Jesus' life (the sixth to the ninth hours), darkness comes over the earth (which Luke explains as a failing of the sun or as an eclipse, which tech-

[18] Of the two attested readings for Luke 23:42, "When you come in your kingdom" and "When you come into your kingdom," the second is probably more original. Later scribes would have been troubled by the realization that the Kingdom of God was not brought about immediately by the death of Jesus and would have shifted the focus to the parousia which is involved in the first translation.

Lucan Passion Narrative

nically is not possible at Passover time), but it does not obscure the confidence of the dying Jesus. His last words are not those of abandonment (Mark/Matthew) or those of triumph (John) but words of trust: "Father, into your hands I commend my spirit." Adapted from Psalm 31:5-6 (especially as phrased in the Greek Bible), these words, like those in which he forgave his enemies, have offered many a way of meeting death in peace. Once again, the first of the followers of Jesus on this path was the martyr, Stephen (Acts 7:59). Luke places the rending of the Temple veil before Jesus' death, not after (Mark/Matthew); for only acts of grace will follow the death of Jesus. The first is a final affirmation of the innocence of Jesus drawn from a centurion, so that timewise on either side of the cross a Roman governor and a Roman soldier have made the same declaration of not guilty. Then the Jewish multitude who followed Jesus to Calvary and looked on (Luke 23:27, 31) is moved to repentance, so that the people return home beating their breasts. A sign of goodness is evoked even from the midst of the Sanhedrin, as Joseph of Arimathea, a saintly member of that body who had not consented to the purpose or the deed of crucifying Jesus, asks for the body of Jesus in order to render the required burial service. If the daughters of Jerusalem wept over Jesus on the way to Calvary, providing the mourning required for burial, the women of Galilee (alongside Jesus' male acquaintances!) look on the burial from a distance (23:49, 55) and prepare spices to complete the burial. The words that will ultimately be addressed to the Galilean women will not be words of warning such as those addressed to the Jerusalem women but words of joy—their burial ministrations will prove unnecessary, for Jesus is among the living, not among the dead (24:1, 5). It has often been critically observed that the cross bears for Luke none of the atoning value that it had for Paul. Lucan crucifixion, however, is clearly a moment of God's forgiveness and of healing grace through and by Jesus. The theological language may be different, but the atoning effects are the same.

The Passion According to John

This passion narrative is read in the liturgy every year on Good Friday, but not without context; for the Johannine Gospel is read daily in the preceding three weeks of Lent and throughout the subsequent Easter Season. Such a context is important for understanding the passion since the Jesus who comes at last to his hour (Jn 13:1) in the Fourth Gospel is a different dramatic character from the Jesus of the Synoptic passion narratives. He is a Jesus conscious of his pre-existence. Through death, therefore, he is returning to a state he has temporarily left during his stay in this world (17:5). He is not a victim at the mercy of his opponents since he has freely chosen to lay down his life with the utter certitude that he will take it up again (10:17-18). If there is an element of struggle in the passion, it is a struggle without suspense, for the Satanic prince of this world has no power over Jesus (14:30); indeed, Jesus has already conquered the world (16:33). Since the Johannine Jesus is omniscient (2:25; 6:6; etc.), he cannot be caught off guard by what will happen in the passion. He had chosen Judas knowing that Judas was going to betray him (6:70-71) and has himself sent Judas off on his evil mission (13:27-30).[19]

A. THE ARREST OF JESUS IN THE GARDEN (18:1-12)

Thus, when the passion scene opens in the garden (18:1), Jesus is not surprised by Judas and the arresting party, as

[19] The reader may be puzzled by my description of the *Johannine* Jesus, since it may resemble the only picture of Jesus he or she has ever known. But that is because it is the Johannine Jesus that has dominated in Christian piety. The Synoptic Jesus does not show any clear awareness of pre-existence, is not so emphatically knowing, etc.

he is in the Marcan account of Gethsemane. Rather he goes forth to meet Judas whom he has been expecting (18:4). And with an ironical touch, John tells us that Judas comes equipped with lanterns and torches. Judas has preferred darkness to the light which has come into the world (3:19); when he left Jesus it was truly night (13:30), and now he needs artificial light. The Jesus who confronts Judas has not been prostrate in the dust of Gethsemane praying that this hour and this cup pass from him, as in the Synoptic tradition; for such an attitude would not be conceivable on the part of the Johannine Jesus. He and the Father are one (10:30); he has specifically rejected any prayer that the Father should save him from this hour (12:27); he is eager to drink the cup the Father has given him (18:11). If there is to be prostration in the dust of the garden, that is the fate not of Jesus but of the Roman soldiers and the Jewish police who come to arrest him. These representatives of worldly power, civil and religious, are struck down when Jesus uses the divine name "I AM" (18:6), in order graphically to show the reader that no one can take Jesus' life from him unless he permits it (10:18). Yet, these soldiers and police have power over Jesus' followers who remain in this world (17:15), and so Jesus protects his own by asking that they be let go (18:8), exhibiting for them a care quite consonant with his prayer in 17:9ff.

B. INTERROGATION BY ANNAS; PETER'S DENIAL (18:13-27)

The Jewish "trial" of Jesus is also quite different in the Fourth Gospel; for it is not a formal procedure before Caiaphas, the high priest, as in Mark/Matthew, but a police interrogation before Annas, Caiaphas' father-in-law. It is an investigation to see whether Jesus admits anything revolutionary in his movement or his teaching (18:19)—

anything that could determine whether Jesus was to be handed over for trial by the Romans. In this interrogation a supremely self-confident Jesus easily outpoints Annas (18:20-21), so that his captors are aggravated to the point of abusing him (18:22). The interrogation leaves Annas, not Jesus, with the embarrassing and unanswered question (18:23).

And while Jesus is showing his innocence, his best-known follower, Simon Peter, is showing weakness. The Fourth Gospel catches the full drama of Peter's behavior, since only here is *Peter* identified as the one who cut off the servant's ear in the garden (18:10). Now he wants to deny that he was even in the garden (18:26-27). Also, the fourth evangelist, more than the others, stresses the simultaneity of Peter's denials and Jesus' self-defense. In 16:32 Jesus had said: "An hour is coming . . . for you to be scattered, each on his own, leaving me all alone." Peter is not yet among those scattered, but he certainly has left Jesus alone.

Again, only in the Fourth Gospel does "another disciple" have a role in the drama of Peter's denial (18:15), presumably "the disciple whom Jesus loved." Whoever he was historically,[20] he was *the* witness par excellence for the Johannine community (19:35; 21:24). If he was someone relatively unknown to other Christian communities, i.e., not one of the Twelve, the fourth evangelist wants all the more to show that his community's patron and hero was present during Jesus' hour of return to the Father (13:1—the Beloved Disciple appears only in chs. 13ff.), at

[20] The late second-century identification of this disciple (never named in the Fourth Gospel) as John son of Zebedee is probably too simplified. More likely he was a companion of Jesus not named in the other Gospels but very important and idealized in the memory of the community whose tradition is preserved in the Fourth Gospel. He had been the model vehicle of the Paraclete/Spirit in bearing witness. For a fuller treatment, see my book *The Community of the Beloved Disciple* (New York: Paulist, 1981).

Johannine Passion Narrative

least, at those crucial scenes at which any other disciple was present: at the Last Supper (13:23-26), in the process against Jesus (18:15-16), at the crucifixion (19:26-27), at the empty tomb (20:2-10), and at the appearance of the risen Jesus (21:7, 20-23). In each scene he is introduced almost as a foil to Simon Peter, the apostolic witness best known to the Church at large; and in each the Beloved Disciple comes off more favorably than Peter. He is quicker to see, to understand, and to believe precisely because he has a primacy in Jesus' love, which is a mark of true discipleship. Thus, the fourth evangelist tells us that his Gospel has behind it a trustworthy and even preeminent authority, a message meant perhaps as a reply to other Christians scandalized by the uniqueness of this community's tradition about Jesus, so markedly different from the Marcan-based Synoptic tradition which was popularly thought to have had Peter as its apostolic authority.

C. ROMAN TRIAL (18:28-19:16A)

When the evangelist turns the stage spotlight from Peter's denials back to the continuing process against Jesus, his scenario for the Roman trial is revealed as a striking artistic conception. This is not at all the Synoptic scenario of a Jesus silent before a Pilate who is interrogating him in the presence of his accusers, the Jewish priests. Rather, it is an elaborate front-and-back-stage setting, with the priests in the crowd outside, Jesus inside, and Pilate shuttling back and forth between them. As he moves from one stage to the other, Pilate is like a chameleon, taking on the different coloration of the parties who engage him. Outside there is ceaseless pressure, conniving, and outcry; inside there is calm and penetrating dialogue. Not at all silent (cf. Mark 15:5), the Johannine Jesus is an eloquent spokesman, answering the false charges of political complicity

Johannine Passion Narrative

that will be brought against his memory during the years to come (not the least by modern fiction writers who want to make him a first-century Che Guevara or by scholars who attribute to him Zealot motives). He will not refuse the title of "The King of the Jews" if Pilate wants to put it that way; but the real reason he came into this world was *not* to be a king (as might be construed from the Jerusalem Bible)—it was to bear witness to the truth (18:37).

So eloquent and self-assured is Jesus that we can scarcely speak of Pilate's trial of Jesus in the Fourth Gospel; it is Pilate who is put on trial to see whether he is of the truth. Pilate may think he has the power to try Jesus, but he is calmly told that he has no independent authority over Jesus (19:10-11). It is not Jesus who fears Pilate; it is Pilate who is afraid of Jesus, the Son of God (19:7-8). The real question is not what will happen to Jesus who controls his own destiny, but whether Pilate will betray himself by bowing to the outcry of the very people he is supposed to govern (19:12). The price he exacts from them by way of an insincere allegiance to Caesar (19:15) is a face-saving device for a man who knows the truth about Jesus but has failed to bear witness to it (18:37-38).

The artistry of the evangelist is never better displayed than in his device of moving the scourging and mockery of Jesus to the center of the Roman trial (19:1-5). In the Marcan/Matthean tradition the scourging was part of the sentence and immediately preceded the journey to Calvary after Jesus had been condemned. The purple cloak in which he was mocked was stripped off before he set out for the place of execution (Mark 15:16-20). But John makes the scourging and mockery a prelude to the climactic moment of having Jesus brought from inside the praetorium to encounter the crowd outside—the mid-moment of the trial, breaking Pilate's shuttle, where all three parties meet in center stage. In all the Gospels the cries to crucify Jesus represent a self-judgment on the part of the onlookers; but no other evangelist highlights the harshness of the cry so effectively as does the fourth evangelist when he makes it a response to Pilate's *Ecce homo.* In its origins "The Man" may reflect an ancient christological title for Jesus, something akin to "Son of Man"; but in the Johannine drama it has had the effect on countless readers of making the rejection of Jesus an action literally inhumane. Moreover, since the Jesus who is rejected wears the mantle and crown of a king, this rejection, combined with preference for Caesar, is portrayed as an abandonment by the Jews of their own messianic hopes.

Here I must beg the reader's indulgence for an aside. One cannot disguise a hostility toward "the Jews" in the Johannine passion narrative, neither by softening the translation to "Judeans" or "Judaists," nor by explaining that John often speaks of "the Jews" when the context implies that the authorities (i.e., the chief priests) alone were involved. By deliberately speaking of "the Jews" the fourth evangelist is spreading to the synagogues of his own time the blame that an earlier tradition placed on the authorities. He is not the first to do this, for the oldest extant Christian writing speaks of "the Jews who killed both the Lord Jesus and the prophets" (1 Thes 2:14-15). But John is the most insistent NT writer in this usage. Why? Because he and/or his confreres have suffered from synagogue persecution. They have been driven out of the synagogue for professing that Jesus is the Messiah (9:22; 12:42). Within a few decades of the composition of John there was introduced into synagogue prayer (*Shemoneh Esreh* or the Eighteen Benedictions) a curse against deviants from Judaism, including followers of Jesus. This was an initial example of an attitude that is still with us today: in the view of many Jews, no matter how true and long one's Jewish lineage may be, one ceases to be a Jew when one confesses Jesus to be the Messiah. At the end of the first century, expulsion from the synagogue seemingly exposed Christians to Roman investigation and punishment, even death—Jews were tolerated by the Romans; but who were these Christians whom Jews disclaimed? The fourth evangelist may well be alluding to this painful outcome in 16:2: "They will put you out of the synagogues; indeed, the hour is coming when whoever kills you will think he is offering service to God." The context of mutual hostility between the Johannine community and the synagogue must be taken into account when proclaiming the Johannine passion narrative in the Good Friday liturgy.[21]

But let us return from this aside to the closing lines of John's account of the Roman process against Jesus. Pilate wrings from the priests a denial of their royal messianic hopes in favor of allegiance to the pitiful Tiberius, brooding on the cliffs of Capri (19:15). After that, Pilate hands Jesus over "to them" (to the priests) to be crucified (19:16a).

D. CRUCIFIXION, DEATH, AND BURIAL (19:16B-42)

There is no Simon of Cyrene in the Fourth Gospel; the Johannine Jesus carries his own cross (19:17) as a continuing sign that he lays down his own life (10:18). The crucifixion in John consists of a series of short vignettes, some of them similar to Synoptic episodes, but now vehicles of peculiarly Johannine theology.

All four Gospels mention that a charge (*titulus*) listing Jesus as a would-be "King of the Jews" was fastened on the cross, but only John sees here the dramatic possibili-

---

[21] See the cautions about preaching on p. 16 above.

ties of a proclamation. Pilate has already presented Jesus to his people as king (19:14), only to have him rejected (19:16). Now, in all the pertinent languages of the Empire, Hebrew, Latin, and Greek (19:20), Pilate reaffirms the kingship of Jesus and does so with Roman legal precision (19:22). In spite of the objection of the chief priests, the representative of the greatest power on earth has verified that Jesus is king for every passerby to see. The Johannine understanding of the crucifixion is beautifully caught by a line that Christians interpolated into Psalm 106:10, a line known already in the second century A.D.: "The Lord reigns from the wood [of the cross]."

The other Gospels make implicit allusion to Psalm 22:19 in describing the division of Jesus' garments; John makes the allusion explicit, but with particular attention to the seamless tunic which was not divided (19:23-24). His free interpretation of the psalm in order to highlight the tunic has suggested to some scholars a symbolism based on the seamless tunic of the high priest (described in Josephus). John would then be presenting Jesus on the cross not only as a king but also as a priest, a theme in harmony with the consecration language of 17:19. Others see the seamless tunic as a symbol of unity.

In the Marcan/Matthean tradition the women who followed Jesus watched from afar; and none of the disciples was present, for they had fled (cf. Mark 14:50). John's picture is quite different. Not only are the women placed at the foot of the cross, but the Mother of Jesus is included among them, together with the Beloved Disciple (19:25-26). These are two figures whom John names only by title (cf. 2:1); they meet at last at the moment of Jesus' death. Each was a historical person, but the evangelist is not interested primarily in their historical identity; he is interested in their symbolism. In Mark 3:31-35 (Matt 12:46-50) when his "mother and brothers" come asking for

him, Jesus asks, "Who are my mother and my brothers?"
He answers this question in terms of discipleship:
"Whoever does the will of God is brother and sister and
mother to me." In John the dying Jesus leaves his natural
mother as the mother of the Beloved Disciple, and that
disciple is designated as her son, thus becoming Jesus'
brother. Jesus has constituted a family of preeminent disciples,[22] and the Johannine community is already in existence at the cross (which becomes the birthplace of the
church).

In 19:29-30 a sponge full of common wine is placed on
hyssop and offered to Jesus, an episode recalling the Mar-
can/Matthean incident where the sponge was placed on a
reed and offered to him before he died. By mentioning
hyssop, fern-like and certainly less suitable than a reed,
John is again playing on symbolism, for in Exodus 12:22
hyssop was used to sprinkle the blood of the paschal lamb
on the doorposts of the Israelite houses. Jesus is sentenced
to death at noon (19:14), the very hour on Passover Eve
when the priests begin to slaughter the paschal lambs in
the Temple precincts. In his death he gives meaning to
that mysterious acclamation of John the Baptist uttered
when Jesus made his first public appearance: "Behold the
Lamb of God who takes away the sin of the world"
(1:29).

For the fourth evangelist even the very human cry "I
thirst" (19:28) must be set in the context of Jesus' sovereign control of his own destiny. Jesus utters it "aware that
all was now finished, in order to bring the Scripture to its

---

[22] Besides being symbolized as the mother of the Beloved Disciple, when the
context of the whole Bible is taken into account, the Johannine figure of the
Mother of the Messiah may evoke *Israel* or Lady Zion, the people of God to
whom the Messiah is born, and *Eve*, the "woman" of Genesis 2:23 and her off-
spring (cf. Rev 12:18).

complete fulfillment." And when he takes the wine, he declares, "It is finished," and he hands over his spirit. How different is this calm scene of Jesus' laying down his life when ready from the tortured atmosphere of the last words in Mark/Matthew: "My God, my God, why have you forsaken me?" And even the formula, "bowing his head, he handed over the spirit" (19:30), may be redolent of Johannine theology. More than the other Gospels John preserves the ancient Christian understanding that the communication of the Holy Spirit, i.e., the Spirit of Jesus, was an intimate part of the death and resurrection. The Fourth Gospel (7:39) is insistent that the Spirit is not a reality for Jesus' followers until then. John dramatizes this by having Jesus breathe his Holy Spirit forth on his disciples (including members of the Twelve: 20:24) as his first act when he appears on Easter Sunday evening (20:22). Here John may be suggesting by way of symbolic anticipation that Jesus handed over his Spirit to his followers at the foot of the cross, in particular to the two followers (the Mother and the Beloved Disciple) idealized by the Johannine community as their antecedents.

If Jesus has died in both a sovereign and life-giving manner, these traits do not disappear from the narrative with his death—the dead body is the body of a king and it continues his salvific work. The latter trait is apparent in 19:31-37. The other Gospels mark Jesus' death with miraculous signs in the ambiance: the Temple curtain is torn; tombs open and bodies of the saints come forth; and an expression of faith is evoked from a Roman centurion. But the Fourth Gospel localizes the sign in the body of Jesus itself: when the side of Jesus is pierced, there comes forth blood and water (19:34). In 7:38-39 we heard: "From within him shall flow rivers of living water," with the explanation that the water symbolized the Spirit which would be given when Jesus had been glorified. That is

Johannine Passion Narrative

now fulfilled, for the admixture of blood to the water is the sign that Jesus has passed from this world to the Father and has been glorified (12:23; 13:1). It is not impossible that the fourth evangelist intends here a reference not only to the gift of the Spirit but also to the two channels (baptism and the eucharist) through which the Spirit had been communicated to the believers of his own community, with water signifying baptism, and blood the eucharist (3:5; 6:53, 63). The added touch that no bone of Jesus was broken (19:33, 36) is seemingly still another echo of the theme of Jesus as the paschal lamb (Ex 12:10).

The burial of Jesus is narrated in all four Gospels, but here once more John goes his own way in order to stress the sovereignty of Jesus. Not only the traditional Joseph of Arimathea but also the exclusively Johannine character Nicodemus appears on the scene. He was attracted by Jesus during the ministry, yet scarcely with enough understanding to make of him a disciple (3:1-10; 7:50-52). Now, when Jesus' disciples have been scattered (16:32), Nicodemus comes forward with courage to perform the burial duties. The words of Jesus are beginning to come true: "When I am lifted up from the earth, I shall draw all men to myself" (12:32). And this is no burial like that in the Synoptic tradition, without anointing and aromatic oils (cf. Mark 16:1; Luke 23:55-56). Rather Jesus is buried as befits a king, with a staggering amount of myrrh and aloes, bound in cloth wrappings impregnated with aromatic oils (19:39-40).

Thus, from beginning to end the narrative has been consistent: it is the passion of a sovereign king who has overcome the world. It is the passion narrative to which the *Vexilla Regis* is the appropriate response.

Diverse Portrayals of the Crucified Jesus

A common position in biblical scholarship today[23] is that the Gospels were the product of development over a long period of time and so are not *literal* accounts of the words and deeds of Jesus, even though based on memories and traditions of such words and deeds. Apostolic faith and preaching has reshaped those memories, as has also the individual viewpoint of each evangelist who selected, synthesized, and explicated the traditions that came down to him.[24] All of this means that while there is one Jesus at the font of the four canonical Gospels, each evangelist knows a different facet of him and presents a different picture. We have seen this verified in an acute way in the different Gospel portraits of the crucified Jesus. Since Matthew differs only slightly from Mark in the passion narrative (at least in portraying the role of Jesus), we can speak practically of three different portraits: those of Mark, Luke, and John. Let me describe those portraits briefly, and then turn to the question of truth.

Mark portrays a stark human abandonment of Jesus which is reversed by God dramatically at the end. From the moment Jesus moves to the Mount of Olives, the behavior of the disciples is negatively portrayed. While Jesus

[23] For Roman Catholics this is the official position of their Church phrased by the Pontifical Biblical Commission in its 1964 statement on "The Historical Truth of the Gospels." For the essential portion of that document, see my *Biblical Reflections on Crises Facing the Church* (New York: Paulist, 1975) 111–15.

[24] In the Biblical Commission document referred to in the preceding footnote a distinction is made between the apostolic preachers who have been eyewitnesses and the evangelists who had to depend on previous tradition. Most scholars, Catholic and Protestant, think that no one of the evangelists was himself an eyewitness of the ministry of Jesus.

Diverse Portrayals

prays, they fall asleep three times. Judas betrays him and Peter curses, denying knowledge of him. All flee, with the last one leaving even his clothes behind in order to get away from Jesus—the opposite of leaving all things to follow him. Both Jewish and Roman judges are presented as cynical. Jesus hangs on the cross for six hours, three of which are filled with human mockery, while in the second three the land is covered with darkness. Jesus' only word from the cross is "My God, my God, why have you forsaken me?" and even that plaintive cry is met with derision. Yet, as Jesus breathes his last, God acts to confirm His Son. The trial before the Jewish Sanhedrin had concerned Jesus' threat to destroy the Temple and his claim to be the messianic Son of the Blessed One. At Jesus' death the veil of the Temple is rent, and a Roman centurion confesses, "Truly this was God's Son." After the cross it is possible, then, to see that Jesus was not a false prophet.

Luke's portrayal is quite different. The disciples appear in a more sympathetic light, for they have remained faithful to Jesus in his trials (22:28). In Gethsemane if they fall asleep (once not thrice), it is because of sorrow. Even enemies fare better; for no false witnesses are produced by the Jewish authorities, and three times Pilate acknowledges that Jesus is not guilty. The people are on Jesus' side, grieving over what has been done to him. Jesus himself is less anguished by his fate than by his concern for others. He heals the slave's ear at the time of the arrest; on the road to Calvary he worries about the fate of the women; he forgives those who crucified him; and he promises Paradise to the penitent "thief" (a figure peculiar to Luke). The crucifixion becomes the occasion of divine forgiveness and care; and Jesus dies tranquilly praying, "Father, into your hands I commend my spirit."

John's passion narrative presents a sovereign Jesus who has defiantly announced, "I lay down my life and I take it

Diverse Portrayals

up again; no one takes it from me" (10:17-18). When Roman soldiers and Jewish police come to arrest him, they fall to the earth powerless as he speaks the divine phrase, "I AM." In the garden he does not pray to be delivered from the hour of trial and death, as he does in the other Gospels, for the hour is the whole purpose of his life (12:27). His self-assurance is an offense to the high priest (18:22); and Pilate is afraid before the Son of God who states, "You have no power over me" (19:8, 11). No Simon of Cyrene appears, for the Jesus of John carries his own cross. His royalty is proclaimed in three languages and confirmed by Pilate. Unlike the portrayal in other Gospels, Jesus is not alone on Calvary, for at the foot of the cross stand the Beloved Disciple and the Mother of Jesus. He relates these two highly symbolic figures to each other as son and mother, thus leaving behind a family of believing disciples. He does not cry out, "My God, why have you forsaken me?" because the Father is always with him (16:32). Rather his final words are a solemn decision, "It is finished"—only when he has decided does he hand over his spirit. Even in death he dispenses life as water flows from within him (see 7:38-39). His burial is not unprepared as in the other Gospels; rather he lies amidst 100 pounds of spices as befits a king.

When these different passion narratives are read side-by-side, one should not be upset by the contrast or ask which view of Jesus is more correct: the Marcan Jesus who plumbs the depths of abandonment only to be vindicated; the Lucan Jesus who worries about others and gently dispenses forgiveness; or the Johannine Jesus who reigns victoriously from the cross in control of all that happens. All three are given to us by the inspiring Spirit, and no one of them exhausts the meaning of Jesus. It is as if one walks around a large diamond to look at it from three different angles. A true picture of the whole emerges

Diverse Portrayals

only because the viewpoints are different. In presenting two diverse views of the crucified Jesus every Holy Week, one on Palm/Passion Sunday, one on Good Friday, the Church is bearing witness to that truth and making it possible for people with very different spiritual needs to find meaning in the cross. There are moments in the lives of most Christians when they need desperately to cry out with the Marcan/Matthean Jesus, "My God, my God, why have you forsaken me?" and to find, as Jesus did, that despite human appearances God is listening and can reverse tragedy. At other moments, meaning in suffering may be linked to being able to say with the Lucan Jesus, "Father, forgive them for they know not what they do," and being able to entrust oneself confidently to God's hands. There are still other moments where with Johannine faith we must see that suffering and evil have no real power over God's Son or over those whom he enables to become God's children. To choose one portrayal of the crucified Jesus in a manner that would exclude the other portrayals or to harmonize all the Gospel portrayals into one would deprive the cross of much of its meaning. It is important that some be able to see the head bowed in dejection, while others observe the arms outstretched in forgiveness, and still others perceive in the title on the cross the proclamation of a reigning king.

Diverse Portrayals

Works of Raymond E. Brown published by The Liturgical Press:

A Coming Christ in Advent (Matthew 1 and Luke 1)
An Adult Christ at Christmas (Matthew 2 and Luke 2)
A Crucified Christ in Holy Week (Passion Narratives)
A Risen Christ in Eastertime (Resurrection Narratives)
A Once-and-Coming Spirit at Pentecost (Acts and John)

The Gospel and Epistles of John—A Concise Commentary
The New Jerome Bible Handbook, edited with J. A. Fitzmyer
   and R. E. Murphy